CAPE POETRY PAPERBACKS

ADRIAN HENRI
PENNY ARCADE

Adrian Henri

PENNY ARCADE

POEMS 1978–1982

JONATHAN CAPE
THIRTY BEDFORD SQUARE, LONDON

First published 1983
Copyright © 1983 by Adrian Henri

Jonathan Cape Ltd, 30 Bedford Square, London WC1

British Library Cataloguing in Publication Data
Henri, Adrian
Penny Arcade.
I. Title
821'.914   PR6058.E53

ISBN 0-224-02140-0

'Harbour' and 'Cat' were first published in
Ambit; 'Dusk Song' was first published in *For
David Gascoyne's Sixty-Fifth Birthday* (Enithar-
mon Press); earlier versions of 'The Business'
and 'New York City Blues' were commissioned
by Radio City, Liverpool.

Printed in Great Britain by
Whitstable Litho Ltd, Whitstable Kent

Contents

I should like to thank the Arts Council of Great Britain for my fellowship as Writer-in-Residence at the Tattenhall Centre, Cheshire, 1980–2, during which time most of these poems were written. Thanks also to Mark Fisher and the staff of the Centre for all their help, and to Jed and Jude. . .

'For the virgin afraid of thunder; for the wife obeyed
by her husband; for the spinster in love with Africa,
    O Bear with the Ragged Staff, hear us.'

                    W. H. Auden, 'The Orators'

I Have Woken This Year

I have woken this year
to the delicate half-light of Devon
to the echoing police sirens of this city
in the innocent white light
of the Cheshire countryside.
And I have woken in her bed in Berlin
in the soft lamplight of dawn on Apo. Paulus -Str.
Woken in a four-poster
huge in a huger room in Cambridge
an old guest
in the Old Guest Room
woken to
the strange brown unexplained stain
on my bedroom ceiling
often with you beside me
our unexplained stains on the brown bedclothes.
I have woken on a train
looking at the breasts of a stranger
pink path across a pale-green cornfield
woken in a hotel room in Würzburg
stained with the faintest pantie-smell
of the daffodil she gave me in Munich
to day through the skylight above your window
– *daydream believer* –
and the shared roselight of a caravan in Malvern.
Woken in Rotterdam
blood staining the morning sky
poems drifting like gossamers from plane trees
to the grey-brown suck of light
on a Thames houseboat.
Woken in a heap
at the foot of my own

green and unHoovered stairs
and woken (worst
of all) amid the remains
of a small bamboo table
and huge jagged moons of glass
Victorian stuffed birds suddenly exposed
to twentieth-century morning
the telephone buzzing
inexplicably in my ear.
And I have woken to my fiftieth year
two thousand, two hundred and something mornings
my fiftieth year to heaven –

. . . fifty years
and moved across the river
one cobbled hillside exchanged
for another cobbled hillside.
That one/grass between red sandstone/echoed
to the cries of coalmen, bawlies, muffinmen,
steps shining with Cardinal
kids slid on trays
in winter. Here
we sip German wine on the step
in spring sunshine
hosts of golden daffodils
on windowsills/night-time echoes
of riot vans/barbecues in backyards
kids' skateboards
clatter the pavement.
I have woken in this street
to palest winter dreamlight
springlight of childrens' voices
sunlight through these yellow curtains
the empty pillow of autumn.

I have woken to all these years

all these places,
woken to so many worlds,
how many more summer mornings?

As if in a Dream

'Then would my love for her be ropes of flowers, and
                                                    night
A black-haired lover on the breasts of day'
            'Black Marigolds', trans. E. Powys Mathers

It is as if in the light of a dream that I see you,
accidentally,
smiling from that doorway.

black marigolds

First Saturday-night feverish flush of kisses
warm vortex of dark irises
lost breathless in the depths of afternoon
dimpled hills hot in this salt oasis
the hollows of your throat smelling of tamarind.

I wake to a metallic buzzing,
a bluebottle trapped in the room,
dozy, aware of your absence,
it circles far above the city streets,
the shattered windows.

One geranium petal
stuck to my green front door
as we leave.

Early October rain
shuffles across the city garden
pattern of first faint light on the window:
in the London basement bed

I warm my hands
at the still summer centre of you.

The wind that has subtracted chimneys
is wiping the slates clean,
blows
your dark-blue spotted dress
showing
cheeky fifties' stockingtops
on the empty promenade.

Silver-pink horizon
rocks imitate sheep. Sheep
imitate rocks. Bushes
huddle like pensioners
round sodden bowling-greens.

Ravenglass sea
lurks in the unseen darkness
like someone behind the childhood door.

I press summer words for you
into notebooks, like flowers.
Find them again
faded as winter.

black marigolds of summer. . .

On the sky above the bed
there are stars like tree-lights,
street-decorations. I reach out, find you,
warm, mysterious, unexpected,
as the childhood rustle of tissue-paper,
unfamiliar woolly shapes in the dark. Your
bodysmell beneath the bedclothes, rich,

elusive as fir trees. The ghosts of loves past,
lovers yet to come, line the mantelpiece,
persistent as Christmas cards. On the carpet
your clothes lie, forgotten as wrapping paper.

Tomorrow the cold, leftover bed served up,
empty as Boxing Day.

Phantom trees
inhabit silent fields:
in the snowfilled dark
ghost telephones ring
in the crevices of the wind.

' . . . drenched in the blood of love'
we confront ourselves
hands   faces   bodies
murderers' masks
in the bedroom mirror.

'I love you as much
as Friday is pig-day' you say
in a letter.
Uncontrollable as words
piglets litter the morning marketplace.

You left behind
among
scrap-heaps, desolate canals,
the concrete underbellies of flyovers,
new streets built over old pavements.

Here the busy river dimples past
brown mirrorbanks
slow suck of wellington fields

the prickling sound of sodden grass
and the brief life of primroses.

Black undersea earth
and tractors turning into spring
beside still lodges

dark obelisk in the abandoned graveyard
filled with daffodils

wallflowers and periwinkles
down the village street.

Eyes dark
above armfuls of midnight daffodils
after Tennyson we lie
on a bed of Daffodil sky.

Singing singing
buttercups and daisies
you walk into the bedroom:
outside a March wind
tears through the May sky
lilacs and alsatians
blossom in city backyards.

'Some freesias for you
all the way from Birmingham
in a fast white coach'
their smell
a haiku left on my doorstep.

marigolds bloom again
November escapades
crowd the summer afternoon.

Wild strawberries hide
inside the darkness of you
my lips stained with their secret juice.

Warm glow of cornfields
warm brick wall
before the orchard
rapid volleys of birdsong
like mortarfire across the valley
I walk the hillside
under constant surveillance by butterflies.

Now you lie
in the Cheshire sun
with no knickers on
speedwell peer
into the shadows of your thighs
daisies
modestly avert their eyes.

Splashing barefoot through streams
across a Devon lane
laughing in warm summer rain.
The raw umber of Thames mudbanks
sings our departure with the creaking tide.

Extract of Ivy,
Orchid, Green Apple,
Peaches and Almonds,
Lemon and Rosemary,
all the bathtime, bedtime
smells of you

The first soft light of day
fills this sunken garden
with the gentle yellow touch

of autumn. Violet against silver
pigeons bedeck the lawns
against a dream of willows
crowned with stone pineapples
and pale crimson roses.

A hill-fort
holds out against the dark,
drumrolls of cloud
unfurl the last flags of daylight.

black marigolds
in the desert of a long-lost summer.

Harbour

for G. P.
            – 'a place to wander in' –

I

and always
a constant
rainbow
as the northern star   rainbow
stretched across
any estuary
and six swans swimming
where
seven colours burn
as you turn
turn with the air at your back
twin seashells at your ears
with no sounds of ocean
swell of seagulls and the harsh cries of tourists

'once more
to this star'

and also
the little boatlights
harbour of your arms
the darkness of your eyes
reflect the bobbing sea
folded to ourselves far
above the rain   the quayside
constant
as this rainbow constant

fixed
this harbour, estuary,
High Holborn, low pavement
cobblestones along canals
gate of darkness
where white breakwaters are
to meet this
once more
rainbow.

2

from the depths
a shipwreck
nervous swell
of harbour-bell
and the chime of waves

in this dark-
blue world
the long
the endless pilgrimage
to dawn
the nightly sacrament
long vigil to daybreak
kneel at this altar
images distilled
by you – product of tides
and touching, moon and madness – the sweet
deep taste of this harbour
fills the empty world
words lie limp
await a final coming

at last
the carnival departs
skeleton and moon-queen walk the silver streets
last of the sun
shining hibiscus of light
dancers inhabit
the throbbing night.

3

occasions past – this time,
these things – the journeys to take
through white paper
more difficult than mist or mirrors
this bleak sunset
over the gasometers the towerblocks
in some other world
that does not know you
does not own you
the girl
in this white page
with seashells at her ears
is no more you
nor was since she appeared here
this black rainbow
not appear behind her
stark words
against no harbour
 – real, remembered –
this page no oily haven
two words
not six swans
this white desert echo the cries of
no seabirds.

4

'and the hue of skin of the figure
was of the perfect whiteness of snow'

and
always to return
to this place
rainbow and rain
and six swans

constant

or other   the folded vision
safe haven   dark harbour
and lights   riding

dancer and drummer
seagull and salt spray
season-song of constellations
black and silver
orange
and pale magenta of willow-herb
starlight of Michaelmas daisies
along embankments
        – 'the cluster of low shrubberies
            the slanting of tall eastern trees' –
one white wing spotlit
against the rising night
outside of
ancient calculations
candle-lit nightmare
of empty passageways

lost
dazzled

blinded by
your eyes
     – 'the scent of the violet,
        the star-mirroring depths
        of lonely wells' –
eclipse
these constellations
constant
'cold with disuse and forgetfulness'
drifting, helpless
in what white night
carried always
towards this kingdom
hardly glimpsed
sphinx of the ice-floes
lost and drowned   all shipwrecked mariners
before this white altar
dark harbour   pilgrimage
into what new dawn
what fortunate landfall
trawl for words
in what warm seas?

emblems of winter –
    hawthorn and rowan tree
    stooped with berries
    crimson provisions
    against a lichened valley
    bonfires   woodsmoke   the smell
    of wet chrysanthemum leaves
    the hiss of city traffic
 – not efface
this time   that place
our footsteps
your face against the streetlights
or summer rain beside canals

the rusty eloquence of the empty pier
or
        once more
this harbour, rainbow
constant
your white coat, pale shell earrings
as the northern star
fixed
proof
against
all armoury
of times, places
body shared with
other faces
on the morning pillow
though
the two foxgloves
in your shadowed hedge
grow
another year
for someone else

constant

not forgotten

proof against dark seasons
    – harsh words, tears
       and telephones, cold
       stranger's eyes across the café table,
       these words
       strewn like autumn
       on the foreign pavement –
to return
always

to this place
this sudden
summer rain
fall
always
through these words

rain

rainbow

swans

constant

dark

harbour

as the light

press
of seabell,
seagull

once more

to

this

white

paper, body,
seashell, raincoat,

constant

swell

these eyes
enfold
this universe.

Seaside

dawn chorus:

Like angels awaiting some fishy nativity
in the lace-curtain light
hosts, perspectives of seagulls fill the sky
shriek and gibber
I lie like leather in whatever stone you choose to set
their raucous cries fill my head
like the sheeted dead
you stir in your sleep
away from me.

2

Gaily painted pleasure-steamers
ply their trade between us
from my headland I scan, anxiously,
the expected messenger is not
in any of their argosies.

3

The sea has carefully mislaid the beach
beyond our reach. It looks like rain.
Over the boardwalk bridge we trace in vain
your lost shell earring – remembered image
of harbour, swans, and rainbow – gone perhaps
back to its watery element.

We examine its green brothers in the Shell Shop
and do not find its like. Its lack
as tangible as absent-minded station kisses.
Your eyes as distant, clouded
as the sea in its remote horizon.

4

We sit on the pier and talk of growing old.
A seagull wheels, agelessly. The sea
moves restlessly from right to left. Before
the fishermen cast their lines. Behind, the dodgem-cars
are tuning up. BINGO. SOUVENIRS. The painted shapes
of clouds unreal as candy floss. The distance gapes
wide as the emerald gap beneath the planks,
between our feet.

5

There was, I remember, something about a harbour.
And, yes, a rainbow and – what was it?
Swans, yes, that was it, swans – laughing
we pass unnoticing the window. Our sepia faces
frozen, helpless.

The Business

It's always men who do you wrong
So why not make them pay?
You'll find a friend who'll put you wise
Why give it all away?

The ship girl

The last one was a Dutchman, the one tonight's a Greek
It's just like being married but it only lasts a week
And then it's down the House of Sin to find another one
I wish I could just sail away and no one know I've gone.

O Brothers tell your sisters
Not to go where I have been
Spending my life with sailormen
Down in the House of Sin.

The massage girl

You'd like to do so many things
Your wife won't understand
Lie down, we'll soothe your cares away
Just leave it in our hands.

The call girl

My grandma walked down Lime Street
And they called her Maggie May

But my name is Michelle
And things are different today.

A contact girl, a contract girl,
With candlelight and wine,
Just dial my number any time
The pleasure will be mine.

The street girl

Upper Parly's cold and wet
It's colder in the Square
I'm here beneath the lamplight
You can always find me there.

When he left me I was six months gone
So what's a girl to do?
I never got my CSEs
All I can do is screw.

It's the oldest game a girl can play
This every woman knows
By day and night, in rain or snow,
The business doesn't close.

In hotel lounge or on the street,
A cabin or a car,
A photo on a glossy page,
You need us: here we are.

Rainbow

Seven Places for Maurice Cockrill

I

Soggy ponies in a New Forest hailstorm
wet almost red bracken. Black line
of cloud to the far horizon, moulting
like cat's fur, sweeping curtains of rain.

Now trees against the sunset, and deer
deep in wet grass and bluebells.
The red mud stiff beneath our feet.

Lyndhurst, Hampshire

2

St Just-in-Roseland: orange lichens on gravestones
dark ramsons massed with white flowers
palm trees campions bluebells primroses
heaped above each other.
Herringbone brick of walls through ivy and young ferns,
berberis and alexanders. Frayed stems of coconut palms.
Grey stone against the brightness of orange-pink azaleas.

St Just, Cornwall

3

Breasts bloom like crocuses in the lunchtime sunlight
underwear blossoms on estates
stern yuccas guard suburban gardens

fishermen sprout beside still lodges
beneath blank hillsides.
In York daffodils flood the walls
and a sweet-voiced girl wears the station sunlight

in her hair.

York

4

Faded confetti under churchyard yew trees.
Willow aslant a brook, haunted
by wild rhubarb. One low curved tree-trunk
mirrors the water. Yarrow and moon-daisies.
Yellow monkey-flowers against pink rocks
in the cool viridian shadows. Above our heads
the moor waits, patiently.

Silvington, Shropshire

5

A blue poem
written with a
blue pen
on a morning of
blue hills
calm brick farmhouses
and children's laughter from the other room.

Tattenhall, Cheshire

6

Fête champêtre: ducks in the dusk,
painted butterflies over painted trees darken to autumn,
lost voices whisper in empty drawing-rooms.

ghost dancers flit past shrouded columns
dusty Sèvres trembles to the sound of the *valse*.

green-painted benches crisp on frosted gravel.
dry leaves crunch under unseen footsteps.

Paris

7

Elm trees stand patriarch
against the violet dark.
Last song of birds
in the birch tree still red
against the darkened sycamores.
Yellow streetlamps deny the light
define the night.

Ham Common, Surrey

September City

September,
season of street accidents
the end of summer loves,
harsh family gatherings,
the death of ancestors.

Cruellest month,
vain anticipations,
false treasures kept in empty wardrobes,
all safely gathered in,
blackberries, the beginning of hollow fruitfulness.

Double agent,
tireless infiltrator,
sunlight on empty promenades,
image seen in a tarnished mirror,
the burning-off of stubble.

September,
season of preparations,
kisses like holiday snaps,
the taste of warm bodies
like mislaid addresses.

September,
time of separations,
tides turn towards the moon,
chrysanthemums at city corners,
children return reluctant to classrooms.

Cruellest season of sunshine and funerals,
mists and ambulances,
bulldozers clearing the debris of summer.

Poems from Germany

'. . . Songs of a wayfarer . . .'

I

Giant hogweed takes over suburban gardens,
unobtrusively,
murmuring of *lebensraum*
VORSICHT BISSIGER HUND
thunders from every gateway,
only the foxglove wanders free;
the evening light
is decorated with oakleaf clusters.

2

Primroses lurk in the darkness of cupboards
the bird has been deflowered, feathers drift
across stained bedclothes. A sad girl
prepares the grave of the last amaryllis
märzebecher   maiglöckchen
the sound of the last train
drowned by the sound of the fountain.

3

GEOFF BOYCOTT we love you
Christopher Isherwood is a fucking liar
written on The Wall
rabbits run free
in the grey Vopo wilderness

body soft in the lamplight
shy voice on the telephone
a small crimson bear
left at Bahnhof Zoo
in the early morning.

4

Perfumdeo/a found poem

Spring dream
Yellow moon
Wild flower
Green summer
Blue river
           (Deodorant names from a supermarket shelf)

5

Dream

The blue dream rises gently from the ground
its pink mouth agape
hovers above the crowd
bumps gently against an ochre dream
drifts towards the sun
which is ringed with rainbows.
           Max Beckmann, 'Der Traum', (1927)

6

You are the tiny onion
given like a pearl

in the crowded lunchtime café
a poem hidden
in the oyster of your smile
while the sun runs amok
in the busy street
drunk on daffodils.

7

I bring you from Germany
tangerine-flavoured lipsalve
called KISS ME
a chocolate hare for Easter
and a pack called, simply,
Anti-Baby Condoms.

8

acrostic

My
Only
Night
In
Köln
Alone.

9

Sunlight on the Alster. A boat called Charly
bobs behind your head. Words left
unsaid. Shade of umbrellas, willows,
a dazzle of green park, thick brush-strokes

on the water. Empty glasses on the orange table.
You teach me to say *zahlen bitte*. Flotillas
of baby ducks. Swans turn, languid as
middle-aged sunbathers, stirring to do the other side.
The minutes to go like the lapping of small waves
as the ferryboat arrives.
            (Würzburg/Siegen/Cologne/Berlin/Munich/Hamburg)

Three Landscapes, Yorkshire

1

Morning fields
rich with buttercup and fennel.
Mysterious armchairs
lichened to stone.
Your cerise dress seen amongst
rhododendrons
in a viridian valley.

2

The valley sighs blue in the afternoon
cuckoos imitate people imitating cuckoos
chimneys shift from foot to foot in the heat
like traffic policemen.

3

Evening:
your pale pink shirt
the columbines outside the window
the sky above the hill
all coloured the same.

Only your eyes
retain the cornflower afternoon.

Adrian Henri's Talking Toxteth Blues

Well, I woke up this morning, there was buzzing overhead
Saw the helicopter as I got out of my bed,
Smelt the smell of burning, saw the buildings fall,
Bulldozers pulling down next door's wall.
      Toxteth nightmare . . .
          . . . yes . . .
             . . . city with a hangover.

Then I remembered what happened last night
The sirens and the shouting and the TV lights,
Banging on the riotshields, petrol bombs in flames,
Cars all a-blazing, shattered window-frames.
      Felt sick to my stomach . . .
          . . . don't cry for me . . .
            . . . Upper Parly.

Saw a busy lying blood pouring from his head,
Saw one stop a paving stone, thought that he was dead.
Heard the sound of engines in the bright orange night,
Saw the headlights blazing, saw the crowd in flight.
      One of them . . .
          . . . didn't run fast enough . . .
            . . . Land Rovers . . .
              . . . . long way from the farm.

Well I saw the Chief Constable up on TV
And the Superintendents, but they never saw me,
Saw the Home Secretary and the Minister for Riots,
And all them social workers who just never keep quiet.
      . . . never met a one of them . . .
          . . . neither did the coppers.

Saw a woman walking in the firelight's glare,
'Hey Aunty Maggy, what you doing there?'
Arms full of liquor and a portable TV,
Said, 'All the rest are doing it, why not me?
　　　. . . do yourself a favour, son,
　　　　　　. . . nice music centre . . .
　　　　　　　　　. . . just over there.'

Well I thought a bit about it and I took her advice
Crowd was having fun and the goods looked nice,
Then a scuffer copped me and they threw me in a van,
Took me off to Risley and the Magistrate Man.
　　　　. . . exemplary sentence . . .
　　　　　. . . act as a deterrent . . .
　　　　　　　. . . law 'n' order . . .
　　　　　　　　　. . . Toxteth nightmare . . .
　　　　　　　　　. . . city . . .
　　　　　　　　　　. . . with a
　　　　　　　　　　　　hangover.

Colden Valley, Early Spring

Frost persists to afternoon
on one side of this valley
icicles depend
the shadow of the other bank
moves inexorably to the diagonal
never allowing the daylight to fall
here.

Rich textures of lichen
green elephant-hide of beeches
palest sienna of bracken
beckon in the March sunlight.

Here there are only stones of purest marble
frozen in small streams.
The brightest afternoon
cannot dispel the darkness
beneath these stunted branches.

Poem i.m. P.G. Wodehouse

Darkness at the Drones Club
dust settles silently on mahogany chairbacks
a ghostly footman shimmers in
black-edged card on a silver salver.

A Wee Scottish Song

(for Paul McCartney)

Listen, hen,
there's nae folk in the glen
nae monsters in the loch
och
but it's dull
in the Mull of Kintyre.

Landscape with Aeroplanes

the sound of a jetfighter
gathers itself across the sky
tears between us
rumbles into insignificance
leaving only our silence
and the housemartin
mimicking its going.

foxgloves reach out, beckon
cow-parsley spread open in supplication
tiny secrets of wild strawberries
known only to butterflies, distant
droning of a tractor, a bird-scarer
regular as the one o'clock gun. Smell
of honeysuckle and the marzipan breath
of meadowsweet, heavy
in the afternoon.

sudden thunderjet

hurls out of the hedge

scattering the rooks who croak
their indignation. Two magpies
flap across a field full of sheep.
distant tors of Dartmoor,
and the sudden apparition of a white cat
at a turn of the lane.

dragging their sound behind them

the jets startle by again.

North Devon

Aubade

I mourn for something that was never there
Remind myself of times a year ago:
The scent of roses in the morning air.

In this small room the senses all declare
You were with me, my love, and yet I know
I mourn for something that was never there.

Mist hides the hills, the season is so unfair,
Left here I sit and watch the summer go,
The scent of roses in the morning air.

Bees can't resist the honeysuckle's snare.
Frantic as they are, clumsy and far too slow
I mourn for something that was never there.

Thoughts of your eyes, the morning in your hair,
Lost like a leaf against the river's flow,
The scent of roses in the morning air.

Time will not stop: your careless hand will tear
The faded snapshot, all that was left to show.
I mourn for something that was never there,
The scent of roses in the morning air.

From a Hollywood Diary

1

'People used to say my place looked you know
comfortable but I wanted it to look artistic you know
artistic kind of. So I took out the Dining Area
and made a kind of gallery wall . . . it's nice here
. . . you want to go to the beach Sunday? OK
. . . it's a deal. Ten o'clock . . . I'll come by for breakfast
. . . OK?'

2

Marina del Rey:

HOME OF TURTLE RACING EVERY THURSDAY NIGHT
the split white skirts of 1940 Acapulco waitresses.

Beyond the freeway, the sagebrush,
the oilpumps nod, patient as donkeys.

3

dust,
ash from the bushfires in the next canyon
skin the pool. Cacti, succulents,
heaped-up palm trees. Silver-blue,
silver-purple, leaves from the Silver Dollar
Eucalyptus pour open-handed on to my notebook,
skim the blue depths.
                Later,
the sky shades blue to green, orange to purple
against the silhouettes of palms. Crescent moon
puny against the fireglow, the bright neon.

VENICE OBSERV'D

pale sand against the dark-green sea
a lone woman practising Tai Ch'i
the black girl in suntop and cutoffs
rollerdances to music only she hears
from the headset in her ears.

A postcard home: 'I've just paddled in the Pacific.
Terrific. Wish you were here.' I munch Pastrami, see
REAGAN NAZI painted on the concrete seawall.

sunlight falls
on YE BIKINI SHOP
RENTA–BIKE
RENTA–SKATE
RENTA–BOARD
the blue maw
gaping white jaws
of THE FISH SHANTY.

sandpipers,
head, feet and beaks
going like clockwork,
play chicken with the breakers
like naughty children.

5

cheeky Chicano girls
from Hollywood High – *où sont*
les Foxy Ladies, *Star Magazine*,

Bowie-eyed teenqueens
d'antan?

6

muscular
hustlers
guard
the S & M
boulevard.

7

'In Southern California the Colonel's got more
Than three hundred kitchens with chickens galore.'
sings the radio.
                    The old folks go
to Plummer Park, talk of the Old Country, play cards
in summer sun. DOG EXERCISE AREA
empty, cyclone-fenced. Dogs exercise
everywhere else. Blue-rinsed old ladies,
trouser-suits bright as azaleas, hurry in bunches
for their welfare lunches.

8

I loved you, missed you, wrote poems for you here
in 1973. Now you sip opposite me
six o'clock cocktail ritual, Carlos 'n' Charlie's,
Barney's Beanery, The Mirabelle. We do not tell
the times between, sweet and bitter
as a Margarita.

47

'And tonight . . .

The taxi. The dark doorway. Sudden curtains.
The blinding light. You do not understand.
This poem is pushed into your hand.
The sound of applause. The smiling compère.
The poem is bound between red leatherette covers.
Pages of glossy photographs. Dates, names, places,
some of which you may
have been connected with.
We have flown 6,000 miles at limitless expense
someone you do not remember. We have not thought
to bring the pale-faced girl
who had the abortion in 1964. Nor
the adopted child happily unaware
in Huddersfield. We have brought
the best man you detest
from the wedding you knew even then was a mistake,
we have brought your bride; she is making every effort
to look happy. Showbiz personalities you may have
rubbed shoulders with, or once visited your town, are here.
Their teeth gleam, sincerity teems
like sweat under the spotlights. Do not fear
this is a happy occasion: the compère says so.
Various elderly relatives are trundled in. The fun can begin
in earnest. He is here, smile at the ready,
the poem held steady. Accent thick
as Irish coffee. Earnest author. Firm announcement.

> . . . gentle reader, this is
> your poem'

Penny Arcade

for Joseph Cornell

Utopia Parkway:
Blind arcades. Bouquets
of shipwreckcd flowers.
Melted majesty of the sunset. *Salsa verde.*
The city from 100 storeys
open to the night. WE HAVE RUSH
shout the walls, the highways.

Utopia Parkway:
Night tide. Beauty convulsive as
eyes lit by sea-light. Outside
the white hotel the stars
are printed in their course.
666 in neon
above the frozen, haloed city.

Utopia Parkway:
Parrots wait
patient as pharmacists. Drifts of dawn
like ice-floes against tall towers.
Miss Jasmine glitterqueen
declares the daylight,
hearts scattered on the broken kerbstones.

A palace of dreams waits untenanted
A parkway of light up the morning street.

New York City

Angler

His waders among the water-crowfoot,
intent behind his sunglasses, he casts repeatedly,
does not see me pass.
                    I sit
on the riverbank, see the meadowsweet,
agrimony, remembered dragonflies,
hear the water break the channel, cast about
for words.
            Later
he trudges past, his creel
empty, sees my empty
notebook, smiles a secret smile
of complicity.

Totleigh Barton, Devon

Dial-a-Poem

a poem
instead of a phone call
a jewel
exchanged
for a green apple
on an empty station
two minutes
of silence
away from the red-framed world
outside

a song
for a kiss
a kiss
for an apple
an apple
for a jewel
a jewel
for a poem
a poem
instead of a phone call
I didn't make
last night.

Canadian Landscapes

1

Mist and mirrors.

Nude stranger peering round the corner:
the divided self in bathroom mirrors.

Tops of glass towers lost in mist.

Black squirrels scurry among yellow leaves
Storm-windows stacked in suburban kitchens.

Toronto, Ontario

2

Pumpkins for sale at the side of the road
a red fire-hydrant in an orange forest
the rich sienna of peeling arbutus
fields of kale iridescent as eucalyptus leaves.

Grey-pink seatrunks, grey-green water
of the sound. Shoals of islands
bask in the morning
sky soaring towards the Pacific.

Victoria, B C

3

Last night they showed us the sunset.
The prairie sky shading to purest green.
Only the lime-green streetlights
remain. Now

it's the dawn
                S
                O
                U
                T
                H
        HughMcColl's
                P
                A
                R
                K
coming up like – if
not exactly thunder – an
angry purple line
hard against the red horizon.

Edmonton, Alberta

4

As I walk this motel
the corridors snarl, shake
with the tread of unseen feet. The elevator
mutters 'trick or treat'.
Grey faces loom
over the shattered ice-machine.
In the gloom of the cocktail lounge
stark muzzles croon
soundlessly.

Regina, Saskatchewan

5

The Northern Lights
rise in the sky, twitch,

descend.
Above
the bungalows
the red steam from an exhaust
the frozen puddles
the huge shapes push
and pull, like shower-
curtains, gently,
gently.

Saskatoon, Sask.

6

LAURA SECORD:
dark chocolates on
a dazzling white counter. A
dark chocolate arm from
a dazzling white sleeve
framed in the doorway.

Yellow lamplight. Two bodies
together on yellow hotel sheets.
Outside, the car brakes, electronic
police-sirens scream
like animals mating.

Montreal, Quebec

7

Huge skies open to sunset,
pale orange of tamaracks,
the sudden interruption of mountains.
POULET FRITE A LA KENTUCKY
armchairs on white verandas

fir trees black against the clear light
fading from blue to green to orange
MOTEL   BONNE CUISINE   COCKTAILS
in the bar Le Georgian Willie and Waylon,
Emmylou and Dolly, sing the night. I wake
to remembered loving,
the dream of a field of dazzling snow.

Lennoxville, Quebec

8

. . . 'The storm of embraces,
The circus of dark departures.'

Christopher Levenson

Sunlight, and the clear chime of bells
in at the open window. Traces of you
still on the pillow, on my body, in this room
far above the neon city. Mist
and mirrors. Above the glass towers
the clouds have got stretch marks.

Toronto, Ontario

Season Song

love
lies buried
like poppyseeds by a motorway
for many an autumn
cold mists
chance meetings
winters of strangers
snow
drifting through conversations

spring
stirs the ground
words not yet spoken
punctuated by crocuses
horse chestnuts bud
hesitant as phonecalls

summer
come at last
celandines bring swallows
words blossom
like meadowsweet
foxgloves in shaded gardens
tears like summer rain
pavements warm as kisses
eyes in the darkness
mysterious as trout streams

now,
in the warm darkness of you
evergreen and deep as forests
we store these words
against a cold season.

For a Feminist Poet

If I tell you I've gone weak
at your knees
will you promise
not to write a poem about me?

. . . and the days grow short . . .

mid-
September
and already
the poems are starting to draw in.

Souvenirs d'Anglesey

Valse

1

the sea,
and first sight of storage-tanks
early blackberries
and a white goat
grazing on a guest-house lawn.

2

pale moon
in an immovable blue sky

bright Pompeiian light
on symmetries of abandoned kilns
votive shapes
of bleached brickwork.

slow
suck
of the tide
perspectives of curlews
and the distant sound of seagulls.

3

double-shaded
rockpools

crimson, viridian
dreams
against slow rhythms
of monotone weed.

4

white sheep
clipped
neat as topiary
three dark-green sandpies
against the sunlit grass.

5

a sprig of weeping willow
from where his brave leg lies buried
in some corner of a foreign field.
Before painted perspectives of a harbour
haunted by sea monsters
the Fifth Marquis (as
Pierrot) waltzes nervously
with one elegant, leather limb.

City Morning

7 a.m.:
I huddle the thought of you to me
like a child's comfort-blanket.

Evensong

I write you poems in dayglo colours.
You hold them against the sunset
and tell me you cannot read them.

At Your Window

proudly I present
a dead mouse
at your window
dismembered birds
at the kitchen door
cannot believe
do not conceive
your horror
at the gifts I bring you.

Morning Landscape, Tattenhall

Two saturated wreaths of poppies
at the foot of the War Memorial.
Behind the drenched coppice, tiny
waterfall, tangled winter branches,
a haunted grange still dreams.
Over the bridge, and two sudden beams
of sunlight from the broken sky
touch the distant hills,
like an Annunciation.

Tattenhall, Cheshire

Dusk Song

Only to drown in the dark of your eyes
eyes that haunt parsonages
that well like the sea on beaches
eyes as warm as August
as lonely as a cricket pavilion shrouded in mist
distant as spaces between the stars.

Only to know you waiting in the boathouse
lap of sea-light on dilapidated walls
lost child on the moors
crying at the blood on the spotless table-cloth
your dreams filled with nightmares and rocking-horses
as you haunt mine.

Only to touch you in dusty hotel rooms
the busy restaurant, the echoing ballroom,
green grass growing everywhere between us.

Only to drown in your eyes like morning
mysterious as duskfall on distant planets
familiar as sunlight and the smell of seaweed.

New York City Blues

for John Lennon

You do not cross the road
To step into immortality
An empty street is only the beginning

The words will still flow through you
Even on this cold pavement,
Are heard in some far place
Remote from flowers or flash-bulbs.

In that city, on Gothic railings
Dark against the snowy park
Still a dead flower, a faded letter,
Already one month old.

'Life is what happens to you
When you're busy making other plans,'
This empty street
Is only the beginning.

Here, in your other city,
Riot vans prowl the December dark,
Remember angry embers of summer,
Familiar ghost guitars echo from stucco terraces.

Meanwhile, in the Valley of Indecision,
We rehearse stale words, store up expected songs,
Celebrate sad anniversaries.
Flowers and flash-bulbs. Cold pavements.

You do not cross the road
To step into immortality
At the dark end of the street
Waits the inevitable stranger.

Cat

Today, up early for a morning train,
I heard it. Distinct and near.
A thin mewing, as of a cat
locked in somewhere. In my ear
as I ate a hurried breakfast.
Was it your familiar voice again?
I do not know. Know only that
in that high sound the past
came flooding back.

Small and black.
                    Fifteen years,
eight poems, three or four paintings.
Not always at the centre of things: an attendant lord,
perhaps, one that will do to start a progress,
swell a scene or two.

The Entry of Christ into Liverpool
                              You
are there, getting under the feet of heroes, friends
some now almost forgotten. You stare
out of the picture. Banners. Distant sounds
of Orange Lodges. Strange
we never really named you.
                         Left behind
by Fred who went to Canada, and
didn't come back. Fierce, tiny, black,
you dominate the house, allow
no stranger animals within.
                        Polished, O-Cedar
floorboards of our top-floor flat. White brick wall,

brass fireplace. You downstairs, 'big-eyed in the hall
for Kit-e-Kat'. Like Caligari you patrol
the crooked roofs of Canning Street. Attic bedroom,
skylight that you leap through, surprising us
to morning. Familiar meals, familiar money-quarrels,
gradual separation. The paved backyard she sunbathed in
exchanged for one a block away.

You stay,

apparently unnoticing.

'Black cat
called my
darling on
a spring day'   (H.H., 2.2.1964)

Rose-bay
willow-herb she pressed in '58
given ten years later, with kisses.
Small poems warm as eggs. Rainbow words
written from Rossendale, tucked in bright blue
envelopes. *Holy Night, Silent Night*
. . . *Really Got a Hold on Me* . . . 'Glad to be
seen with you' . . . Brown stockings, dark-blue
sneakers, suspender belt. First snow, cold hands
in Piccadilly Gardens. White
Christmas loudspeakers.

Forlorn sound,
a thin high
mewing. Perilous seas,
faery casements.
By the desk,
a photograph,
two frozen strangers. Times preserved
only in poems,
like aspic.

66

No
madeleine and lime tea
but sausages and coffee
and that elusive noise
again.

1968 and summer gone.
Hands held in parks and palm-houses,
backstage and bedsits,
gone with first frost. All our spring
ending.

Worried letters to me in the USA.
You have run away, come back,
won't eat. She writes perpetually
of diets started and abandoned, hers
and yours. Films she's seen, the *Beano*,
'Coronation Street', the house (this house)
we're buying. Crying at being alone.
Long-distance voice on the telephone.
Enormous in your winter coat, plagues of fleas
in summer.
           The freezing fog
that changes Princes Road
into a dreamworld for her. Cobwebs,
dandelion clocks.
                Now moved here
and six months ill. Measured-out tiny meals,
the pills. Waiting for her sound along the street,
at the door, morning and evening, your warmth
curled against the bedclothes at my feet.
Then the time
              I put a child's toy necklace
round your neck at Christmas. Artificial pearls

in the light by the kitchen door. Your face
against the glass. Come in from a party, she thinks
the toad who lives in the grid by the corner
has changed you into a Princess.
                                        How
you'd pump your claws, relentlessly,
when happy, dribble on people's laps, scrabble
at scraggy plants where lilies last
in the sun-starved backyard bloom'd.

          Un Déjeuner sur l'Herbe her
spread naked across two canvases
above the picnic ham, salami, sliced watermelon.
Derek and me, his black-and-white dog
behind her in a Shropshire garden. Long grass,
lichened stone, a shock of nasturtiums.
                              You sit among them
there in the foreground, stare from the picture
again.
                              Screwing
on the settee can't wait in the hallway dark-
green Pre-Raphaelite 'Sunday dress' naked
beneath the folds, the smell of her, the sight
of white breasts in that green-shaded bower;
glimpsed thicket as she leans above me.
                                                  You,
perched on the arm, watch, unblinking.
                              Afterwards,
wet patch on the Morris print, we wonder
what you're thinking.

Now,
the thin high mewing comes again
sharp and insistent as the remembered taste
and smell. What stories you could tell.

Late autumn. Dead chrysanthemums

RELATIONSHIP COMPLETELY DESTROYED
Black November claims responsibility

                              near,
clear as the sound of traffic or milk bottles.

          The humpbacked bridge by her friends' house
where we used to meet. The morning street,
the prison wall, the time a ball came over it,
fell at her schoolgirl feet. Poems in her every
letter. Butterflies in the dark of pillarboxes.
The aching bridge, white platform
of separation.
                    Seven years since
and somehow still together.
                              Cold sidewalks of New York,
warm pavés of Paris. Hampstead Sundays,
Normandy mornings.
                    Shared poems,
often for others.
                    Typewriter from the top floor,
telephones. Summer coffee on the step
by the front door.
                    You, of course, insist
on sitting on the newspapers
we want to read.
                    Two years now
since that bright walk in the morning
sun. Going for milk and papers,
she found you. Dead
in Hope Street. Not injured,
not run over, just lying
on the May pavement.

So whose voice now, so close to ear?
What plaintive sound? Ghost cat
shut in what phantom cupboard?

Our morning rituals, wordgames, who
makes the drinks, dream conversations
no longer include
the feeding of you.
                         Forgotten
hangover smell of catfood.

Like summer rain. Glimpsed rhododendrons
from a train. Met in a foreign city,
the last one never knew you. Gone now,
too.

                              No more
panic keys for someone to feed you,
let you out and in.
                         Once left you
locked out for a week.
                              Your frantic squeak
of hunger, welcome.
                              Finish the coffee,
check the key, close the door quietly
behind me.
                    Down the steps, the tiny sound
not quite gone away.
                              Throbs grey the city day.
Dull bell of awakening, distant smell
of burning.   .
              A helicopter caught overhead
like a bluebottle.

Not enough fragments
shored up against these ruins:
undisciplined squads of words
riotous assemblies of sentences
hurl petrol-bombs, hack at riot-shields,
smoke looms from blazing paragraphs,
streets of looted volumes. Headaches
hang above the burnt-out cars,
the ruined cinema.

                Pavements
mutter of dole, complain of headlines,
chip-papers.

              Last echo

of that small
voice.

              Memory.

A thin high
mewing.

             It comes,
                   again.